PERSISTENT PRAYER JOURNAL

Discovering God's Will for Your Life

JOELLA G. SIMMONS

WESTBOW
PRESS®
A DIVISION OF THOMAS NELSON
& ZONDERVAN

WestBow Press books may be ordered through booksellers or by contacting:

WestBow Press
A Division of Thomas Nelson & Zondervan
1663 Liberty Drive
Bloomington, IN 47403
www.westbowpress.com
844-714-3454

Scripture taken from the King James Version of the Bible.

ISBN: 978-1-6642-5434-3 (sc)
ISBN: 978-1-6642-5435-0 (e)

Print information available on the last page.

WestBow Press rev. date: 01/14/2022

This journal is for women and young girls to help them strength their faith and to show them how God uses ordinary people to complete his plans.

Dedicated to the memory of my mother, Bernice Simmons who I use to hear praying everyday for her children. She was a woman of strong faith and in spite of the many obstacles she endured, she was able to maintain her strength and faith in the Lord.

"I will praise thee; for I am fearfully and wonderfully made ..." Psalms 139:14

This Prayer Journal has resources that give you the opportunity to have a solid foundation in your Christian walk. If you study and complete the worksheet you will see that God created, you to fulfill a destiny that will exceed the expectations of any you could plan for yourself. He provided you with the means to complete your call through His Son Jesus. When you accepted Jesus as the Way the Father provided for you to form a kinship relationship with Him, you receive the same benefits of sonship that Jesus has. You can not create the type of future you want without the Father and Jesus.

CONTENTS

Developing a Quiet Time

- If you want God's blessings in your life, you need to spend time with Him on a consistent basis, praying and devoting time to the Word.
- Find a consistent place and time in which you can be relatively undisturbed.
- Get a translation of the Bible you understand.
- Begin with a simple daily reading schedule.
- Ask the Holy Spirit to increase your understanding. Begin by asking the Holy Spirit to remove any doubts you may have and to teach and lead you in all truth (John 16:7–13).
- Meditate on scripture. When a passage stands out, ask yourself the following questions:
- What does it mean?
  - ✓ How does it apply to me?
  - ✓ Who wrote the book of the Bible I am reading?
  - ✓ Why did He write?
  - ✓ What kind of person did He write it for?
  - ✓ What are the words saying to the people they were writing to?
- Keep a record in this journal of thoughts, questions, and anything that comes to mind.

When you meditate on the Bible, you use all the gifts that God has given you, including

- your mind, so that you may understand;
- the eyes of your imagination, so that you may see;
- the ears of your heart, so you may hear God speaking to you;
- your memory, so that God's words may heal, comfort, and strengthen you;
- your feelings, so you may respond to God emotionally; and
- your will, so that you can set yourself to follow God's purposes.

The Holy Spirit Helps Us

- The Holy Spirit give us the gift of prayer. He also helps us to use this gift. He is able to do this because, as Jesus said, "He is our counselor" (John 14:26) the word *counselor* means "comforter" or "advocate"—someone who knows how to help another person when he or she is in need. We are invited to ask for the Holy Spirit's help whenever we pray.

- In Paul's letter to the Romans, he says, "The spirit himself testifies with our spirit that we are God's children" (Romans 8:16).

- The Holy Spirit helps us with our praying. Paul's scripture says, "We do not even know what we should pray for nor how to pray as we should; but the Holy Spirit prays for us. And the Father who know all hearts knows what the Spirit is saying as He pleads for us in harmony with God's own will" (Romans 8:26–27).

- The Holy Spirit prays in us, for us, through us, and with us. We never pray alone but always in partnership with the Holy Spirit.

Praying and Discovering God's Will

Prayer is an honest conversation with God.

Prayer is my spiritual lifeline.

- Jesus is my mediator and high priest. Through Jesus I have direct access to God. "For there is one _, and one __ between God and men, the man_" (1 Timothy 2:5).

Prayer is an expression of my needs, and God invites me to ask, even though He already knows what my needs are.

- "Ask, and it shall be _ you; seek, and ye shall __; knock, and it shall be __ unto you" (Luke 11:9).

What do I pray about? Everything.

- "Be careful for nothing; do not worry about anything but in __ by _ and supplication with thanksgiving let your _ be made known unto God" (Philippians 4:6).
- I will be earnest and sincere, as God knows and sees my heart before He hears my words.

Why Pray?

- Prayer is a form of worship.
- As a child of God, it is my privilege to go directly to God with my needs, my requests, and my thanksgiving.
- "God is a spirit; and they that _ Him must worship Him in _ and in _" (John 4:24).
- Prayer develops a habit of close fellowship with God.
- It preserves me from evil. "And lead us not into temptation but deliver us from evil" (Matthew 6:13).
- It brings forgiveness. "If we confess our sins He is faithful and just to _ us our sins" (1 John 1:9).
- It secures me, strengthens me, and gives me personal guidance.

How Do I Begin a Prayer?

Address prayer to "my heavenly Father" with respect. Some other titles may be "our Father," "gracious Father in heaven," "our loving God," and "dear Lord."

What Should My Prayer Include?

Prayer should include

- praise, adoration, and thanksgiving; an outpouring of gratitude to God because of His grace, mercy, and loving-kindness;
- communion (Luke 6:12; 1 John 1:3);
- confession of sins and wrongs (Psalm 51:1–10);
- petitions (pleas for personal help; Philippians 4:6);
- intercession (petition on behalf of others; Romans 9:1–2); and
- submission (Luke 22:42).

Praise to God—The Importance of Praise

- Worshipping God is what we do in acknowledgement of God's excellent being. Praise describes our attitude toward what God has done, while worship is offered for who God is.
- All believers are commanded to praise God! In fact, Isaiah 43:21 explains that praise is one reason we were created.
- Praise originates in a heart full of love toward God. Deuteronomy 6:5 says, "Love the LORD your God with all your heart and with all your soul and with all your strength."

Praise to God—How to Praise God

- Praise can be expressed in song, in Bible verses, or in prayer, and it is to be done continuously. Psalm 34:1 instructs, "I will [extol] praise the LORD at all time; His praise will always be on my lips."
- Praise to God is expressed outwardly through our everyday actions, as well as inwardly in our thoughts.
- Praise God for His holiness, mercy, and justice (2 Chronicles 20:21).
- Praise God for His grace (Ephesians 1:6).
- Praise Him for His goodness (Psalm 135:3).
- Praise God for His kindness (Psalm 117).
- Praise God for His salvation (Ephesians 2:8–9).

"Truth about You" Scriptures: Scriptures in the Bible to Learn God's Truth about You!

1. God values you (Colossians 3:12).
2. God will complete the work He started in you (Philippians 1:6).
3. God has a good plan for your future (Jeremiah 29:11–13).
4. You are beautiful in Christ (Isaiah 61:1–6).
5. Beauty comes from within (1 Peter 3:4).
6. God's grace is the only thing perfect within you (Ephesians 2:8–9).
7. Christ has appointed you to do His good work (Ephesians 2:10).
8. You are part of God's family (Ephesians 1:4–5).
9. Everyone struggles (Romans 7:21–24).
10. Godliness training is needed daily (1 Timothy 4:8).
11. God requires submission to authority. (Romans 13:1–2).

Revelation of Truth Prayer

Take time to write a prayer, asking God to reveal His truth to all who seek Him.

Trust in the Lord with all your heart and lean not on your own understanding, in all your ways acknowledge Him and He will direct your path. (Proverbs 3:5–6 KJV)

Committed Heart

God is looking for a fully committed heart, not perfection. Read and write down the first sentence of 2 Chronicles 16:9. Meditate on this.

_____

_____

_____

_____

_____

_____

_____

_____

_____

_____

_____

God longs to bless you. He longs to hold you and give you the desires of your heart if you will only worship and serve Him. In order to serve God, you should take time each day to ask Him what He wants you to do. You also should sacrifice your time, energy, and resources for God, and then stand back and watch how God multiplies everything you give Him.

God has great plans for you, but He wants you to understand what it means to believe His truth with your whole heart. When God comes first, you will find real joy in your daily activities of life.

Infinite Blessings

Below is a list of infinite blessings that we have as children of God! As you read this list, ask yourself if you truly believe these things.

- I am the light of the world (Matthew 5:14).
- I am Christ's chosen friend (John 15:15).
- The Lord is my Shepherd; I have everything I need (Psalm 23:1).
- I am chosen and appointed by Christ to bear His fruit (John 15:16).
- I am one of God's holy people (Ephesians 1:4).
- I have an inheritance from God (Ephesians 1:4).
- I have been blessed with every spiritual blessing (Ephesians 1:3).
- I am created in the image of God (Genesis 1:27).
- I am holy and dearly loved (Colossians 3:12).
- I have incredibly great power from God (Ephesians 1:19).
- I have a wonderful future (Ephesians 1:18).
- I am precious, honored, and loved (Isaiah 43:4).

Belief in God

We need to believe in our heads who God is and what He promises us in His Word. We need to believe with our hands by serving God and by following His commandments. Most importantly, we need to believe and trust God with our lives.

Take time to read 2 Timothy 3:1–7. Describe in your own words the meaning of verse 7.

_____

_____

_____

_____

_____

_____

_____

_____

_____

_____

_____

_____

_____

_____

_____

_____

_____

God's Ways

God's ways are not always easy to determine, but He is faithful to show us His path as we seek Him. He will never mislead us as we daily seek to know Him.

What does Ecclesiastes 11:5 tells us about God's ways?

_____

_____

_____

_____

_____

_____

_____

_____

_____

_____

_____

_____

_____

_____

_____

_____

_____

Your Emotions

God never changes; your emotions change! A way to overcome this obstacle in loving God is to always acknowledge all your feelings to Him. God does care about your emotions. He has seen every tear you have cried from the day you were born. He wants to hear about your sadness, anger, disappointments, fears, joy, and desires. Any loving father is interested in what his children are feeling.

Read and write down Hebrews 13:8.

_____

_____

_____

_____

_____

_____

_____

_____

_____

_____

_____

_____

_____

_____

God's Plan for Your Life

Have you ever thought about God's specific plan for your life? If so, write it down.

And do not conform to this world but be ye transformed by the renewing of your mind, that ye may prove what is that good and acceptable, and perfect, will of God. (Romans 12:2)

_____

_____

_____

_____

_____

_____

_____

_____

_____

_____

_____

_____

_____

_____

_____

_____

_____

_____

_____

_____

Your Identity in Christ

What have you learned that may assist you in making your identity in Christ have an impact on you every day?

Before I formed you in the womb, I knew you. (Jeremiah 1:5 KJV)

_____

_____

_____

_____

_____

_____

_____

_____

_____

_____

_____

_____

_____

_____

_____

_____

_____

What God Says Is True

How do you think you would be blessed by God for believing what He says is true of you? I will instruct you and teach you in the way you should go, I will guide ye with my eye. (Psalm 32:8)

Record Mercies of God

Confess any doubts and unbelief you may have. Read Jeremiah 10:19; 23 11:18-20, 14:7, Thus, when Jeremiah was distressed, he reflected on previous mercies. So remember and record the mercies of God in your life's prior situations. Trust God because He is faithful. (Write them down)

Write a prayer thanking God for His faithfulness, mercy, and goodness to you.

Deborah – her name means "Honey Bee"

Her Character: Her vision of the world was shaped not by the political situation of her day but by her relationship with God. Though women in the ancient world did not usually become political leaders, Deborah was just the leader Israel needed – a prophetess who heard God and believed Him, whose courage aroused the people, enabling them to throw off foreign oppression.

Her Sorrow: that her people had sunk into despair because of their idolatry, forgetting God's promises and the faith of their ancestors.

Her Joy: That God turned the enemy's strength on its head, bestowing power to the weak and blessing the land with peace for forty years.

Scriptures: Judges 2; 1-23, Judges 4 - 5

Jael – her name means "A Wild or Mountain Goat"

Her character: - Decisive and courageous, she seized the opportunity to slay an enemy of God's people.

Her Joy: To be highly praised by Deborah and Barak for her part in a decisive victory.

Scripture: Judges 4-5 KJV

Read Judges 2 (KJV)

Judges 2 demonstrates a spiritual pattern that is repeated over and over throughout the book. The term "judge" is from the Hebrew word, shophetim, whose root means "to put right, and so to rule." That is exactly what the judges did during this period. An important lesson about the Christian life is found in the book of Judges, and it is: "Victory is not my overcoming sin, or the devil, or the world. True, lasting victory is only found when Jesus overcomes me." The battle was with Israel wandering even though they knew what God had done for them.

1. What did Israel do that reflected the "sin cycle" as seen in Judges 2 and when did they do it (v.1)?

_____

_____

_____

_____

_____

_____

2. What did the Lord allow to happen, and what part of the cycle does it represent (v.2)?

_____

_____

_____

_____

_____

_____

_____

_____

_____

_____

_____

3. What did the sons of Israel do, and how long did their oppression last (v.3)?

_____

_____

_____

_____

_____

Judges 4 (KJV)

1. Read Judges 4:6-7 and make note of what you learn from Deborah concerning the details of God's plan as she shared it with Barak.

_____

_____

_____

_____

_____

_____

_____

2. What is Barak's response to Deborah, and why do you think he responded that way (4:8)?

_____

_____

_____

_____

_____

_____

_____

3. What was Barak afraid of (4;8)? Why would having Deborah along alleviate those fears?

_____

_____

_____

_____

_____

_____

_____

4. How does Deborah respond to Barak's request (v. 9)?

_____

_____

_____

_____

_____

_____

_____

5. Look at Judges 4:12-13 and write down what Sisera di when he learned there was an army from Israel headed his way.

_____

_____

_____

_____

_____

_____

_____

6. What characteristics does Deborah have?

_____

_____

_____

_____

_____

_____

_____

_____

7. How do you think the Israelite men felt about the honor for this victory going to Deborah and Jael?

_____

_____

_____

_____

_____

_____

_____

8. How did God accomplish this great victory (4:15)? Compare Judges 5:4-5.

_____

_____

_____

_____

_____

_____

_____

9. Use three adjectives to describe Sisera. Think about the fact that he was running away from the slaughter of his men. But also think about the fact that he was the sole survivor.

_____

_____

_____

_____

_____

10. Use three adjectives to describe Jael. Pick adjectives based on Judges 4:17-20.

_____

_____

_____

_____

_____

11. What made Jael able to do what she did? Fear? Bravery? Desperation? How much did the more brutal culture she was a part of have to do with her actions?

_____

_____

_____

_____

_____

_____

12. Why do you think Deborah praised Jael for such a savage deed?

_____

_____

_____

_____

_____

13. What is the ultimate lesson behind the story of Deborah and Barak and Jael and all of the deeds woven with in it?

_____

_____

_____

_____

_____

_____

The Song of Deborah Judges 5

Deborah and Barak sang a song of praise thanking the Lord for his continual love and protection.

1. **What does Deborah call herself in this verse? What does this tell you about Deborah? (Judges 5:7)**

   _____

   _____

   _____

   _____

   _____

   _____

   _____

   _____

   _____

   _____

2. **Why do you think that God chose Deborah as a Judge?**

   _____

   _____

   _____

   _____

   _____

   _____

   _____

   _____

   _____

   _____

LESSONED LEARNED:

- The key to victory was due to the fact that Deborah and Barak did what God told them to do.
- God does not want nor need our help – what He longs for is our trust and our obedience.
- Deborah and Barak stepped out in faith and on God's timing.
- God uses whoever He wants when He wants to complete His plan.

_____

_____

_____

_____

_____

_____

_____

_____

_____

_____

_____

_____

_____

_____

_____

_____

_____

_____

_____

_____

Miriam – Her name means "Bitterness"

Her Character: She showed fortitude and wisdom as a young girl. A leader of God's people at a crucial moment in history, she led the celebration after crossing the Red Sea and spoke God's word to his people, sharing their forty-year journey through the wilderness.

Her Sorrow: That she was struck with leprosy for her pride and insubordination and was denied entry into the Promised Land.

Key Scriptures*: Exodus 2:1-10; 15:20-21; Numbers 12:1-15

Read Exodus 2:1-10 (KJV)

Moses was born to Amram and Jochebed of the tribe of Levi. Hebrews 11:23 tells us that it was "by faith" that Moses' parents hid him, not fearing the consequences of the king's edict. Exodus 2:1-10 states Miriam's role in Moses' rescue from death.

- What was Miriam's part to play in the rescue attempt for Moses?
- When did she approach Pharaoh's daughter (v. 6-7)
- What do you think would have happened to Miriam if their plan were discovered?

Read Exodus 15:19-21 (KJV)

1. **Describe what you think Miriam and the other women of Israel were thinking and feeling as they walked through the red Sea. After they made it safely through, why do you think they chose to dance to express their praise?**

_____

_____

_____

_____

_____

_____

_____

_____

_____

2. How do you think you would have felt in that situation? Would you have danced? Or would you have used some other form of praise to God?

_____

_____

_____

_____

_____

_____

Numbers 12:1-15 (KJV)

Miriam and Aaron Oppose Moses

3. **What do you think Aaron and Miriam had against Moses "Cushite" wife? Do you think his wife was the real problem? What was the real problem, the real reason for their attack?**

_____

_____

_____

_____

_____

_____

4. **Contrast what verses 1-2 reveal about Miriam and Aaron with what verse 3 reveals about Moses. In what ways are you like Miriam and Aaron? How are you like Moses.**

_____

_____

_____

_____

_____

_____

5. In verses Numbers 12:4-9 the Lord appears in the pillar of cloud to Moses, Aaron and Miriam. He then singles out Aaron and Miriam and speaks to them. Why is he so angry with them?

_____

_____

_____

_____

_____

_____

_____

6. In Numbers 12:10-13 why do you think Miriam was singled out for the punishment of leprosy and not Aaron?

_____

_____

_____

_____

_____

_____

_____

_____

7. How do you think Miriam's punishment affected Aaron?

_____

_____

_____

_____

_____

_____

_____

_____

8. Have you ever been in a situation where one person was punished for the wrongdoing of several? How did that make you feel?

_____

_____

_____

_____

_____

_____

9. What do you think Miriam was feeling and thinking when she was outside the camp for those seven days? What would go through your mind if you were in Miriam's position?

_____

_____

_____

_____

_____

10. Even when we are forgiven, we sometimes still have to pay the price for our sins. What sin have you had to pay a penalty for? Do you consider yourself forgiven, even though the effects of your sin remain?

_____

_____

_____

_____

_____

Miriam's story offers an extraordinary example of God's willingness to offer forgiveness to those who sin. Though she had to pay the consequences for her actions – seven days of exclusion from the camp and from all those who loved her – she reentered the camp a forgiven woman.

The position Miriam held: Exodus 15:20-21

After Israel's miraculous deliverance from Pharaoh's army through the Red Sea Miriam is identified as "Miriam the prophetess." She is also described as "Aaron's and Moses sister. She was view as a leader especially by the women since she led them in praise and worship (dancing and playing the tambourine). In Micah 6:4 Miriam is listed as one of the leaders along with her brothers Aaron and Moses. She is the only female mentioned because of her significance in the life of Israel.

Notes for reflection:

- Moses married a foreigner and God warns the Israelites not to intermingle with foreigners because they could turn their hearts to other gods. This did not happen in Moses' case.
- Exodus 7:7 Aaron was three years older that Moses so Miriam would have been the first born and Moses the baby in his family. It could be that both Miriam and Aaron were jealous because they felt since they were older than Moses that they should have maintained an exclusive leadership role.
- Numbers 11:16-17, and 24-30 describes what happened in the leadership structure of Israel and how it affected Miriam's attitude. Up until this point Moses, Aaron, and Miriam had been the sole leaders in Israel. Now Miriam and Aaron have been bypassed in favor of these seventy newly appointed elders who had prophesied (Miriam's argument that the Lord had spoken through her and Aaron as well). They would still have a leadership role, but it would no longer be an exclusive one. Miriam viewed these seventy newly-appointed elders and prophets as a threat to her position while Moses saw them as a much-needed asset.

Lessons learn:

Miriam proved to be one of the great women among the people of God, but she had to learn to trust and follow God according to His ways, not hers. In Numbers 12:4-16 states how God dealt with Miriam and Aaron disobedience. God lets them know that he has a special relationship with Moses that is different and there is no equality of service or consequences for their rebellion. Aaron became submissive and accepted responsibility for his own sin after the Lord rebuked him, but Miriam was prideful and rebellious that is why she was struck with leprosy for seven days.

God disciplines those he loves, every child who belongs to him.

If we confess our sins, God will forgive us.

God's anger lasts only for a moment but His favor lasts forever.

Lot's wife character: She was a prosperous woman who may have been more attached to the good life than was good for her. Her story implies that she had learned to tolerate the sin of Sodom and that her heart had become divided as a result.

Scriptures: Genesis 18:16-19:29; Luke 17:28-33

Read Genesis 19:1-8 (KJV)

Lot's son-in-laws laugh at him – Why! How do you handle people who ridicule your sincere attempts to show them an escape route?

_____

_____

_____

_____

_____

1. Lot invited these men to stay in his home without even consulting his wife. What life style do you think Lot's wife must have made for him and his children?

_____

_____

_____

_____

2. What is the danger of being quiet and how can that hinder or help our relationship with God?

_____

_____

_____

_____

3. What do you think of Lot's suggestion that he give his daughters to the raiders rather that his guest? What reaction do you think Lot's wife might have had?

_____

_____

_____

_____

4. Why would Lot offer such a thing? Keep in mind that according to ancient culture in opening his house to these guests Lot guaranteed not only their comfort but their safety.

_____

_____

_____

_____

5. Why did God spare Lot and his family? Did they deserve such grace?

_____

_____

_____

_____

_____

_____

_____

_____

_____

_____

_____

_____

_____

Read Genesis 19:15-17, 26 (KJV)

Lot and his wife and daughters had three warning from the Angels to flee for your life, don't look back and don't stop?

1. **Why do you think Lot hesitated? What might he have been thinking?**

   _____

   _____

   _____

   _____

2. **Even though warned not to do so, Lot's wife could not resist looking back. Why do you think she turned? Was she sad? Scared? Curious?**

   _____

   _____

   _____

   _____

3. **In Lot's wife, we can see ourselves looking back, regretting decisions made, mourning lost opportunities, yearning for ended relationships. Because we are looking behind us, we cannot see what is before us. We may not turn into a pillar of salt, but we will end up stuck in one place. In Luke 17:28-33 Jesus warns us not to be like Lot's wife. How can we leave the past behind, enjoy the present, and plan for the future?**

   _____

   _____

   _____

   _____

   _____

   _____

   _____

Read Luke 17:28-33 (KJV)

Lessons learned from Lot's wife

- **Actions speak louder than words**
  Lot was in the end, obedient. But for all her silence, when decision time came, Lot's wife disobeyed. The Lord can handle our questions. What grieves his heart is our poor choices. **"The Lord is a God who knows, and by him deeds are weighed."
  1 Samuel 2:3**

- **When God says walk, walk!**
  The angels gave clear commands. So does God's written Word. The Lord already knows the best decisions for our lives. When he shines a light on the path by His Spirit and hands us a map in His Word, let's stop hesitating and start walking!

- **The escape route is clear: Jesus Christ.**
  The Lord uses Lot's wife story to make a point. When he returns, we are to be ready to follow without hesitation, forsaking everything. Salvation is offered freely but at a price; our old lives in exchange for new lives in Christ. His grace has no limits. … except time. Since we know neither the day nor the hour the question is, could we drop everything and go right now?

- **Stuff is temporary. Life in Christ is eternal.**
  **"What good will it be for a man if he gains the whole world yet forfeits his soul?'
  Matt. 16:26**

Rahab – her name means **"Storm", "Arrogance", "Broad", or "Spacious"**

Her character: Rahab was both clever and wise. She saw judgment coming and was able to devise an escape plan for herself and her family. As soon as she heard what God had done for the Israelites, she believed, risking her life in an act of faith.

Scriptures: Joshua 2:1 – 21; 6:17-25; Matthew 1:5; Hebrews 11:31; James 2:25

Read Joshua 2:1-24 (KJV)

Rahab and the Spies

1. How did Joshua's spies happen to meet Rahab?

_____

_____

_____

_____

2. What do you think prompted Rahab to hide the Hebrew spies? Why would the house of a prostitute be a good place for the spies to go when they entered the city?

_____

_____

_____

_____

_____

_____

_____

_____

_____

_____

_____

3. Though the mission of the spies was supposed to be covert, somehow their secret was discovered, and the king of Jericho came searching for them. Read Joshua 2:2-7 and briefly summarize what you learned.

_____

_____

_____

_____

_____

_____

4. To protect the lives of the two spies, Rahab lied to the soldiers sent to her by the king. Was she wrong to do this?

_____

_____

_____

_____

_____

5. Although Rahab was a prostitute, what good characteristics did she have?

_____

_____

_____

_____

_____

_____

6. What evidence of faith do you see in verse 9?

_____

_____

_____

_____

_____

_____

7. What had she heard of the God of Israel (v.10)?

_____

_____

_____

_____

_____

_____

8. What was her response (v.11)?

_____

_____

_____

_____

_____

9. What request did she make of them in return for hiding them from the king's men (vs. 12-13)?

_____

_____

_____

_____

_____

10. Why do you think the spies were willing to deal with Rahab, their lives in exchange for hers?

_____

_____

_____

_____

_____

11. Why do you think God would choose to use someone like Rahab?

_____

_____

_____

_____

_____

12. What does this say about the people God choose to use today to further his kingdom?

_____

_____

_____

_____

_____

_____

_____

13. James mentions Rahab in his plea for believers not to forget that works are an important outgrowth of faith. How did Rahab's actions demonstrate this truth?

_____

_____

_____

_____

_____

_____

_____

14. What lessons in obedience and faith can you learn from Rahab?

_____

_____

_____

_____

_____

_____

_____

_____

_____

Read Joshua 6:17-25 (KJV)

1. What were Joshua's instructions about the city and Rahab (v.17)?

_____

_____

_____

_____

_____

_____

_____

2. What did the people do to Jericho (vs. 21, 24)?

_____

_____

_____

_____

_____

_____

_____

_____

3. Who rescued Rahab and her family, and where did they take them (vs. 22-23)?

_____

_____

_____

_____

_____

_____

_____

_____

4. **What happened to Rahab after the battle was over (v. 25)?**

_____

_____

_____

_____

_____

_____

Rahab's Demonstration of Faith

Rahab is more certain of God's coming deliverance than the spies are. She says, "I know that the Lord has given you the land …" She had heard of God's miraculous deliverance at the Red Sea, which wiped out Pharoah's army and robbed Egypt of its military might. She knew of the Israelite victory over the Amorites, who were destroyed when they opposed Israel. Rahab concluded that the God of the Jews was the one true God. Because she believed in God, she had already cast her lot with His people against her own king, and now she asked that when they came to destroy Jericho, they would spare her and her family.

To guarantee her protection, Rahab **first** must tie a scarlet cord in the same window she had lowered the spies from. She must also stay in her house and hide her family there as well. **Second**, anyone who ventured outside the house would not receive its protection. **The third** condition was that she must not tell anyone about the spies. This symbolizes Rahab faith because she not only believed but she had to put it in action by following the spies' directions.

The Genealogy of Jesus the Messiah

1 This is the genealogy[a] of Jesus the Messiah[b] the son of David, the son of Abraham:

2 Abraham was the father of Isaac,

Isaac the father of Jacob,

Jacob the father of Judah and his brothers,

3 Judah the father of Perez and Zerah, whose mother was Tamar,

Perez the father of Hezron,

Hezron the father of Ram,

4 Ram the father of Amminadab,

Amminadab the father of Nahshon,

Nahshon the father of Salmon,

⁵ Salmon the father of Boaz, whose mother was Rahab,

Lessons learned from Rahab

Our past does not determine our future.

Rahab is remembered because of her bravery not her pass. In the end she was blessed with a good husband in Salmon, an honorable son in Boaz, and a useful place in God's kingdom not because she "deserved it" but because God is faithful and extended grace to her.

Rahab cared about her family's safety, not merely her own.

It does not state if her family believed in God but she still loved them and provided for them in her house.

Obedience often requires public confession.

When Rahab hung the scarlet cord out her window, exactly as the spies commanded her, she marked herself. She did not blend in with her new people – she stood out. Also, she was not afraid to wave her red flag. Sharing with others our past and God's glorious grace does not bind you to your past – it frees you from its power to hurt you any longer.

Let the redeemed of the Lord say this ... Let them give thanks to the Lord for His unfailing love and His wonderful deeds for men. Psalm 107:2, 8

Faith that's demonstrated is remembered.

James chose Rahab as a good example of someone who walked her talk, who put feet to her spoken faith.

_____

_____

_____

_____

_____

_____

_____

Ruth – Her named means "Friendship"

Her Character: Generous, loyal, and loving, she is strong and peaceful, able to take unusual risks, dealing actively with the consequences.

Key Scripture: Ruth 1:4:13-17

Naomi - Her name means "My Joy" or "Pleasant"

Her Character: Suffering is a threefold tragedy; Naomi refused to hide her sorrow or bitterness. Believing in God's sovereignty, she attributed her suffering to his will. But her circumstances, both past and present, led to hopelessness. A kind and loving mother-in-law, she inspired unusual love and loyalty in her daughters-in-law.

Key Scripture: Ruth 1; 4:13-17

Read Ruth 1:1-22 (KJV)

1. **Describe what you think the family of Elimelech and Naomi may have been like. Keep in mind the meanings of their names: Elimelech ("my God is King"), Naomi ("pleasant"), as well as the meaning of their hometown, Bethlehem ("house of bread")**

   _____

   _____

   _____

   _____

   _____

2. **Choose three or four words you think would describe what Naomi experienced in verses 3-5.**

   _____

   _____

   _____

   _____

   _____

3. What do verses 8-18 reveals about the relationship that Naomi and Ruth had?

_____

_____

_____

_____

_____

_____

_____

_____

_____

4. Was the Lord at fault for Naomi's circumstances (1:20-21)? Was He at fault for her bitterness over them?

_____

_____

_____

_____

_____

5. What is more important in life: your circumstances or your reaction to them?

_____

_____

_____

_____

_____

_____

_____

_____

_____

Read Ruth 2 (KJV)

6. According to Ruth 2:1-2, how did Ruth respond to the circumstances in which she and Naomi found themselves?

_____

_____

_____

_____

_____

7. What do you find about Boaz in Ruth 2:1, 4?

_____

_____

_____

_____

_____

8. How did Boaz treat Ruth according to Ruth 2:8-9?

_____

_____

_____

_____

_____

9. What was the testimony Boaz had heard about Ruth according to Ruth 2:11-12?

_____

_____

_____

_____

_____

_____

10. What is Ruth known for? What reputation goes with her to the field?

_____

_____

_____

_____

_____

11. In Ruth 3:3-4, what does Naomi tell Ruth to do?

_____

_____

_____

_____

_____

12. When Boaz was sleeping at the threshing floor instead of at home, was Ruth's behavior immoral? What was she asking Boaz by her behavior?

_____

_____

_____

_____

_____

_____

_____

_____

13. How did Boaz respond and what did he say about Ruth in vs.3:10-11?

_____

_____

_____

_____

_____

14. **According to Ruth 3:12-13 what was Boaz' commitment to Ruth?**

_____

_____

_____

_____

_____

_____

_____

_____

NOTE: Boaz recognized and mentioned Ruth reputation as "a woman of excellence," the same word that is used to describe the virtuous wife of Proverbs 31:10.

Read Ruth 4 to see how God had bless Ruth for her love and commitment to Naomi.

Lesson learned from the book of Ruth

- God uses very ordinary people to fulfill His extraordinary purposes.
- We see the hand of God at work in every situation working to accomplish His purpose.
- By turning our lives over to God we can have security and significance.
- Don't let our circumstances cause us to have a bad attitude about life.

Printed in the United States
by Baker & Taylor Publisher Services